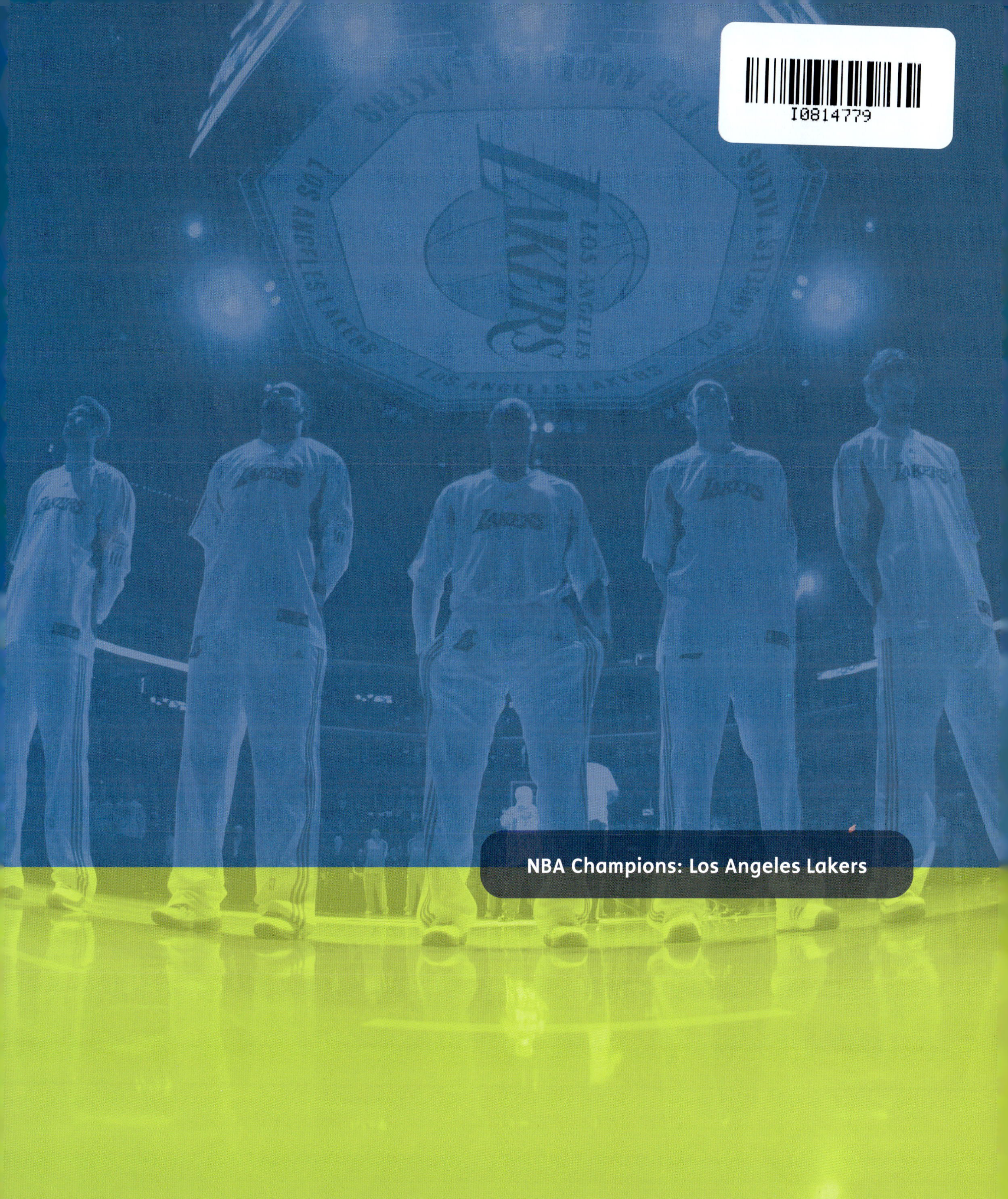

NBA Champions: Los Angeles Lakers

Center Wilt Chamberlain

NBA CHAMPIONS

LOS ANGELES LAKERS

JAMES BARRY

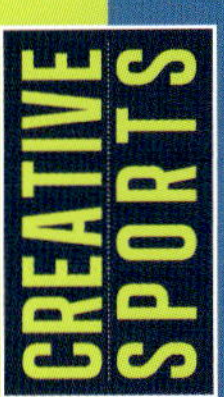

CREATIVE EDUCATION / CREATIVE PAPERBACKS

Center George Mikan

Published by Creative Education and Creative Paperbacks
P.O. Box 227, Mankato, Minnesota 56002
Creative Education and Creative Paperbacks
are imprints of The Creative Company
www.thecreativecompany.us

Art Direction by Tom Morgan
Book production by Graham Morgan
Edited by Grace Cain

Images by Getty Images/Andrew D. Bernstein, cover, 16, 24, George Long, 2, 15, Icon Sportswire, 20, NBA Photos, 4, 12, Noah Graham, 1, Richard Mackson, 19, Thearon W. Henderson, 7, Wally Skalij, cover, 6; Jeff Lewis/Icon SMI, 3; Newscom/ Jim Ruymen, 5, John W. McDonough/Icon SMI 500, 10; Unsplash/Cedric Letsch, 9

Library of Congress Cataloging-in-Publication Data

Names: Barry, James (author of children's books), author.
Title: Los Angeles Lakers / by James Barry.
Other titles: Creative sports: NBA champions.
Description: Mankato, Minnesota : Creative Education and Creative Paperbacks, [2025] | Series: Creative sports: NBA champions | Includes index. | Audience: Ages 7-10 | Audience: Grades 2-3 | Summary: "Elementary-level text and dynamic sports photos highlight the NBA championship wins of the Los Angeles Lakers, plus sensational players associated with the professional basketball team such as LeBron James"—Provided by publisher.
Identifiers: LCCN 2024014026 (print) | LCCN 2024014027 (ebook) | ISBN 9798889892588 (library binding) | ISBN 9781682776247 (paperback) | ISBN 9798889893691 (ebook)
Subjects: LCSH: Los Angeles Lakers (Basketball team)—History—Juvenile literature. | CYAC: Los Angeles Lakers (Basketball team)—History.
Classification: LCC GV885.52.L67 B37 2025 (print) | LCC GV885.52.L67 (ebook) | DDC 796.323/640979494—dc23/eng/20240403
LC record available at https://lccn.loc.gov/2024014026
LC ebook record available at https://lccn.loc.gov/2024014027

Printed in China

Center Shaquille O'Neal

Shooting guard Kobe Bryant

CONTENTS

Home of the Lakers

Los Angeles, California, is the second-largest city in the United States. Many television shows and movies are made there. It has an **arena** called Crypto.com Arena. The Los Angeles Lakers basketball team plays there.

Guard Magic Johnson

The Los Angeles Lakers are a team in the National Basketball Association (NBA). They play in the Pacific Division. That's part of the Western Conference. Their biggest **rivals** are the Los Angeles Clippers, Sacramento Kings, and Boston Celtics. All NBA teams want to win the NBA Finals and become champions.

Minneapolis Lakers 1953

Naming the Lakers

The team began in Minnesota. There are over 10,000 lakes in the state. The team won many championships in its first home. The owner kept the name when the Lakers moved west to California.

Lakers History

The Lakers began playing in the NBA in 1948 in Minneapolis, Minnesota. They were hard to beat. Star center George Mikan was 6-foot-10. He was so good that people called him "Mr. Basketball." He helped the Lakers win five championships in six seasons!

The Lakers moved to Los Angeles in 1960. Smooth-shooting guard Jerry West led the team to the NBA Finals seven times in a row. But the Lakers lost each time. They finally won their first **title** in Los Angeles in 1972.

Point guard Jerry West

Guard Magic Johnson

Point guard Earvin "Magic" Johnson led a fast-moving offense in the 1980s. He helped the team win five championships in the decade. Pat Riley coached Los Angeles to four of those titles. Johnson won three **Most Valuable Player (MVP)** awards with the Lakers.

The Lakers returned to the top in the 2000s. Superstar guard Kobe Bryant thrilled fans with his hot shooting. He once scored 81 points in a game! He led the Lakers to another five titles.

Other Lakers Stars

The Lakers have always had great centers. Wilt Chamberlain stood tall in the early 1970s. Then Kareem Abdul-Jabbar arrived. He became the NBA's all-time best scorer. Giant Shaquille O'Neal was a powerful man in the middle for eight seasons.

Center Kareem Abdul-Jabbar

Forward LeBron James

In the summer of 2018, LeBron James joined the Lakers. Then the team added another great big man, Anthony Davis. James and Davis led the Lakers to another title in 2020. James went on to break Abdul-Jabbar's all-time scoring record. Could the Lakers become champions for an 18th time before he retires? Lakers fans sure hope so.

About the Lakers

First season: 1947—48

Conference/division: Western Conference, Pacific Division

Team colors: purple, gold, and black

Home arena: Crypto.com Arena

NBA CHAMPIONSHIPS:

1949, 4 games to 2 over Washington Capitols

1950, 4 games to 2 over Syracuse Nationals

1952, 4 games to 3 over New York Knicks

1953, 4 games to 1 over New York Knicks

1954, 4 games to 3 over Syracuse Nationals

1972, 4 games to 1 over New York Knicks

1980, 4 games to 2 over Philadelphia 76ers

1982, 4 games to 2 over Philadelphia 76ers

1985, 4 games to 2 over Boston Celtics

1987, 4 games to 2 over Boston Celtics

1988, 4 games to 3 over Detroit Pistons

2000, 4 games to 2 over Indiana Pacers

2001, 4 games to 1 over Philadelphia 76ers

2002, 4 games to 0 over New Jersey Nets

2009, 4 games to 1 over Orlando Magic

2010, 4 games to 3 over Boston Celtics

2020, 4 games to 2 over Miami Heat

TEAM WEBSITE:

https:/www.nba.com/lakers

Glossary

arena—a large building with seats for spectators, where sports games and entertainment events are held

Most Valuable Player (MVP)—an honor given to the season's best player

rival—a team that plays extra hard against another team

title—another word for championship

Coach Phil Jackson

Index